AMAZON PRIME

GET YOUR MONEY'S WORTH FROM PRIME SHIPPING, INSTANT VIDEO, MUSIC, AND THE KINDLE LENDING LIBRARY

By Steve Weber

Published by Stephen W. Weber
978-1-936560-26-4

Free and Discount Kindle books, all you can eat!

Kindle Buffet is a daily website that features a hand-picked list of great Kindle books being offered free that day. Includes mysteries, romance, science-fiction, horror, non-fiction and more. Today's bestsellers and yesterday's classics. You may never need to pay for a book again! See for yourself by visiting www.KindleBuffet.com

kindle buffet!

Free and bargain books, all you can eat!

Page 1 | Page 2 | Page 3 | About / Privacy | Past Issues | My Books

Free Kindle books & bargains for Friday, May 22, 2015

3 Sleuths, 2 Dogs, 1 Murder (The Sleuth Sisters)

Contemporary Fiction
Author: Maggie Pill
FREE

3 Sleuths 2 Dogs 1 Murder MAGGIE PILL

When Retta's "gentleman friend" is accused of murder, the Sleuth Sisters take on the case. Winston Darrow is a charmer, but his secrets create trouble that spills onto Retta, Barb, Faye, and even police chief Rory Neuencamp. Someone is out to get Win, someone he claims is the real killer. While Retta admits Win is less trustworthy than her daffy Newfoundland dog, she insists he's not a murderer.

Dogs become an issue when Faye rescues a mutt she finds hurt on the road. Though Barb isn't a fan, she can't refuse Faye's request to keep the homely, ill-tempered Buddy. Retta, though doubtful about adopting strays, is determined that Faye's dog and her Styx will be

Small Space Organizing: A Room by Room Guide to Maximizing Your Space

Crafts, Hobbies & Home > Home Improvement & Design
Author: Kathryn Bechen
Regularly $12.99, Today $0.99

While we may admire the spacious rooms in large homes we see in magazines or on TV, let's face it: most of us don't live in rambling estates. Instead, we live in homes, apartments, or condos with small rooms and even smaller closets. But you can enjoy an organized, beauty-filled life no matter what the size of your space. In this practical book, you'll learn how to

perform a room-by-room audit of your space to see if it's functioning at its best make

Contents

1 ► Introduction

Way back in 2005, I received an email from Amazon.com announcing a new program called "Prime." It was a simple proposition: If I paid $79 a year for the annual membership, I'd get free two-day shipping on most of my orders. Plus, I could upgrade to overnight shipping at a huge discount—just a few dollars per order.

I'm plenty thrifty, but Amazon didn't need to twist my arm before I coughed up my $79 fee for a Prime membership. It was a no-brainer. I order something from Amazon at least once or twice a week—books, groceries, electronic gadgets (the list has grown every year). So I didn't need to scribble the numbers on the back of an envelope to see that my annual Prime membership would pay for itself within a few months. Easily!

In the decade since then, Amazon has increased the Prime membership fee just $20. Meanwhile, the company has stacked up more and more benefits to Prime, much beyond the special shipping deals that attracted me at the start:

- Free on-demand streaming of movies and TV shows. The service, called Amazon Instant Video, is similar to Netflix's online video service. And while Amazon's video store doesn't yet match Netflix's selection, Amazon is gaining rapidly.
- Free monthly rentals of popular Kindle ebooks, thanks to the Kindle Owners' Lending Library. Anyone with a Kindle device and a Prime membership qualifies for the freebies, up to one book per month, with no due date.
- A personalized streaming music service that might render CDs and radios obsolete.

Whether you're like me—someone for whom Amazon Prime is a must-have—or a more infrequent Amazon customer—this book will explain how to get the most bang out of your Prime bucks.

Since you're reading this book, you probably have several questions about Prime—what it is, and how to use it best. Let's get started:

Which of my Amazon purchases qualify for Prime shipping?

Any item displayed on Amazon accompanied by the Prime badge, ✓Prime, qualifies for free two-day shipping and reduced-cost overnight shipping. In some cases, the same item is offered by multiple vendors (Amazon hosts many independent sellers), some of whom may offer the item at Prime, and some who may not. Sometimes none of the vendors, including Amazon, offer Prime shipping on a particular item, and you'll need to consider various shipping fees quoted by the vendors.

You'll need to order your Prime item by a certain time of day—there's a cutoff time, late in the afternoon, when the two-day window is extended another 24 hours. And in some cases, orders worth more $1,300 require a signature—so if you're not home when the delivery person arrives, you'll need to arrange a different pickup or dropoff time.

What happens if a Prime-eligible item is out of stock?

Then you'll get the customary two-day shipping whenever the item arrives back in stock. If the wait for your item is unbearable, you can cancel your order.

Will my entire order qualify for Prime?

Products that qualify for Prime display the Prime badge, ✓Prime, on the product page and at checkout. If only some of the items in your shopping cart are Prime-eligible, you'll be charged the displayed shipping fee for the ineligible items.

Amazon Prime Details

Free Two-Day Shipping:

Qualifying items:

- Items sold by Amazon.com that are marked on the product page and at checkout.
- Over 100,000 eligible items on AmazonSupply.com.
- Many items that are fulfilled by Amazon.

Qualifying Addresses:

- Nearly all addresses in the continental U.S., except those marked as ineligible below.

Free Standard Shipping:

Qualifying items:

- Items fulfilled by Amazon that are regulated as hazardous materials.
- Items fulfilled by Amazon with special shipping characteristics such as large treadmills, basketball hoops, televisions that are 48" or larger, and heavy furniture.

Qualifying Addresses:

- Addresses in Alaska, Hawaii and Puerto Rico (3-7 business days).
- P.O. Boxes in the continental U.S.
- APO/FPO addresses with U.S. ZIP codes.

Ineligible:

Items:

- Items fulfilled by Amazon Marketplace sellers.
- Magazine subscriptions.
- Personalized gift cards.
- Any item that doesn't have a message indicating that it's eligible for Prime on its product page.

Addresses:

- Addresses in the U.S. territories, possessions, protectorates (other than Puerto Rico)
- International destinations

....

What are the details on the Prime 'Free Trial' offered by Amazon?

You may sign up for a 30-day free trial, during which you'll enjoy all the benefits of regular Prime members. You'll need to have a current, valid credit card registered to your Amazon account. You can't use payment options like a checking account, pre-paid credit cards, gift cards, an Amazon business card, or Amazon line of credit.

To sign up for the Prime free trial:

1. Visit the Prime signup ebpage, bit.ly/PrimeSignup .
2. Click **Start my free trial**
3. Follow the on-screen instructions

Unless you stop it, your Prime trial membership will be automatically upgraded to the paid plan at the end of your trial. To prevent your membership renewal, visit End Your Membership webpage, bit.ly/EndPrime .

Can I share my Amazon Prime benefits with family members?

Yes. Free or paid Prime members can share their shipping benefits with as many as four other family members in the same household. To manage sharing your Prime membership:

1. Visit the Manage Prime Membership webpage, bit.ly/ManagePrime .
2. Click **Invite a household member**.
3. Share your membership by entering the name, relationship, birthday, and email address of the person you'd like to share the membership with.

> Amazon is also very generous about letting you send Prime shipments to family and friends. I've shipped Prime orders to dozens of friends and associates who aren't Amazon customers. This perk isn't unlimited, though. If Amazon determines that you're using the Prime shipping benefit to resell items you've bought on Amazon, your membership may be cancelled.

If my Amazon Prime account is for a business, can I share the benefits with co-workers?

Yes. If you bought your Prime membership for a small business, as many as four co-workers can shop with the same corporate account. Other Prime benefits like Instant Video and the Kindle Owners' Lending Library can't be shared.

I'm a student. Can I pay a discounted rate for Prime?

Yes. Amazon Student members pay $49 a year. Unlike regular Prime memberships, you can't share a student membership with family members or others. Student memberships can last a maximum of four years. After graduation, you'll be upgraded to a regular Prime membership.

How can I cancel my Prime membership?

You can cancel a paid or trial Prime membership in the same place on Amazon's website—the **Settings** section in **Your Account**.

1. Go to the Mange Your Prime Membership webpage, bit.ly/ManagePrime .
2. Complete one of these actions:
    - To cancel a paid Prime membership, click **End membership**. (Paid members who haven't placed a Prime-eligible order receive a full refund.)

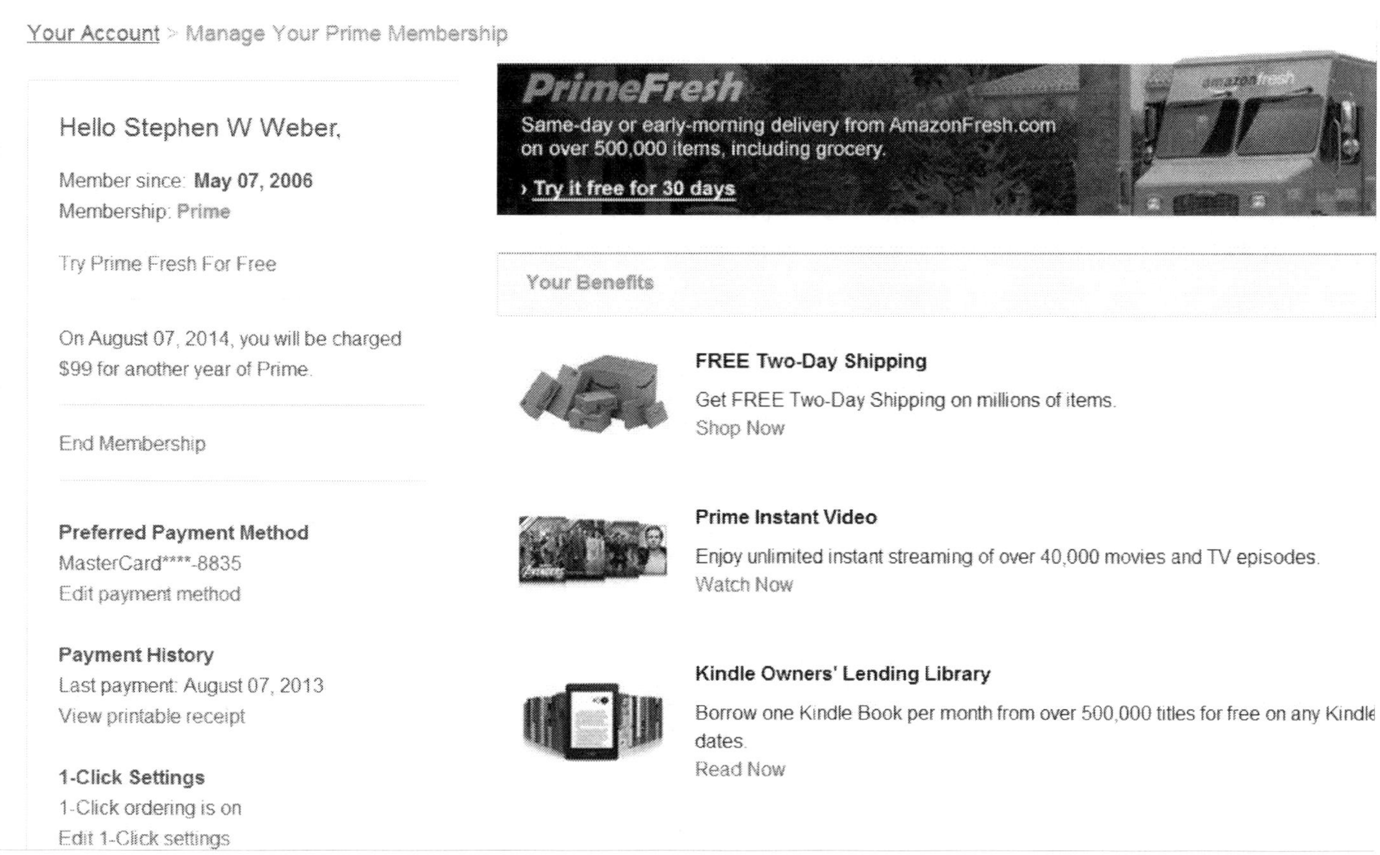

- To cancel a Prime free trial, click **Do not continue**. (If you don't cancel your trial, you'll automatically be upgraded to a paid membership at the end of your trial. The date is listed on the left-hand side of the Manage Your Prime Membership page.)

What is Amazon Mom?

It's a membership program aimed at helping parents and caregivers with young children save on baby, maternity and kid products. Anyone responsible for caring for kids is eligible—moms, dads, grandparents and caretakers. New members are eligible for a three-month free period, which includes free two-day shipping on Prime items, 20 percent off diapers and wipes, a 30-day trial of Prime Instant Video, and other promotions offered to parents. To start the free trial, visit http://bit.ly/MomTrial .

At the end of the free trial, Amazon Mom members pay $99 per year to receive the benefits mentioned above, plus:

- Unlimited instant streaming of thousands of movies and TV shows.
- A Kindle book to borrow for free each month from the Kindle Owners' Lending Library.
- Other Prime benefits, including the ability to invite up to four household members to share your Prime shipping benefits for free.

There's a maximum of one Amazon Mom membership per household.

Can I sign up for Amazon Mom if I'm already a Prime member?

Yes. If you're already a Prime member and you sign up for Amazon Mom, you'll receive all Amazon Mom benefits for no additional charge. If you cancel your Prime membership, you won't receive the Amazon benefits anymore.

What kind of videos can I watch for free?

Amazon Instant Video provides on-demand streaming of movies and TV shows. You can watch them on a Kindle Fire tablet, an iPad, a computer, an Amazon Fire TV, or several compatible TVs and game consoles. As a Prime member, you have free access to a portion of this video catalog. Eligible videos are designated by a "Prime" badge. To view the available videos, visit the Prime Instant Video page, bit.ly/FreeAmazonVideo .

Can I use 1-Click payment with Amazon Prime?

Yes. If you have 1-Click activated, you'll see special buttons on the product pages for Prime-eligible products showing your shipping options. For example, you'll usually see special buttons for **One-Day 1-Click** and **Two-Day 1-Click – FREE**. When available, you'll see a third button for **Saturday Delivery** or **Local Express Delivery**.

If your default shipping setting at www.amazon.com/youraccount is **Standard Shipping**, Amazon will automatically apply free two-day shipping to eligible items when you check out with 1-Click. If you check out using Amazon's shopping cart instead of 1-Click, the shipping speed will default to free two-day shipping for eligible Prime items.

Can I upgrade the shipping to be faster than two-day delivery?

Yes. The tables below show the shipping options:

Addresses in the Contiguous U.S.

One-Day Shipping:

Price varies by item size and weight - as low as $2.99 per item

Saturday Shipping:

Price varies by item size and weight - as low as $7.99 per item

Same-Day Delivery* (in qualifying cities):

$5.99 per shipment

Release-Date Delivery(on qualifying items):

Free

Note: If available, Saturday or Sunday delivery will be specified on the product page and/or during checkout.

*Same-Day Delivery used to be called "Local Express Delivery."

Addresses in Alaska, Hawaii, and Puerto Rico

Expedited Shipping (2-5 business days)

Price varies by item size and weight - as low as $5.99 per item

Priority Shipping (1-4 business days)

Price varies by item size and weight - as low as $11.99 per item

---

Why are many food items ineligible for Prime shipping?

Large, heavy and bulky items (and many small items) aren't a good fit for Amazon Prime because the shipping and labor costs make the items a money-losing proposition for Amazon. To make it economically feasible, the company often bundles items together. But you probably don't want to buy a dozen bottles of hair shampoo at once, even if it is a good deal, do you?

Fortunately, Amazon has figured out a better system for customers who purchase groceries and other household items online: **Prime Pantry**, which is available to Prime members, including Amazon Mom and Amazon Student members.

How does Prime Pantry work?

To make grocery shopping a viable offering, Amazon's Prime Pantry program uses special boxes that can hold up to 45 pounds (or four cubic feet) of household products. When you select Pantry items for purchase—the eligible items are accompanied by a badge, PrimePantry—you'll see what percentage of a Pantry box it fills based on its size and weight. You can buy as much or as little of any item you want, and you pay a flat rate of $5.99 per Prime Pantry box. The boxes are delivered via ground shipping, and usually arrive within four business days.

You'll see Prime Pantry-eligible items as you shop on Amazon.com, or you can visit a separate site dedicated to Pantry items, bit.ly/AmazonPantry .

In the illustration below, you can see an example of a Prime Pantry order is progress. The box has seven items in it, and is 19 percent full. Double-tap to enlarge the picture.

Can I give someone else an Amazon Prime membership as a gift?

Yes. The recipient will get the customary Prime benefits. Gift memberships cost $99 plus sales taxes where applicable. Recipients don't need to enter any credit card information to redeem the gift. For more information, go to bit.ly/AboutAmazonPrime .

2 ► WATCH PRIME INSTANT VIDEO

With your Prime subscription, you can stream Amazon Instant Video movies and TV shows on any compatible device signed into an Amazon account. Compatible devices include computers, TVs, DVD players, home theaters, game consoles and many portable devices.

You can use Amazon's web-based Video Finder to browse categories of videos based on your viewing history. You may discover it's easier to find videos by browsing Amazon's website and saving titles to your Watchlist (simply click Add to Watchlist from the video's description page. Then you can easily browse your Watchlist using another device, such as your home theater or tablet. A link to your Watchlist appears on the homescreen of the Instant Video store.

To watch Amazon Instant Video titles, from the description page, click **Watch Now**.

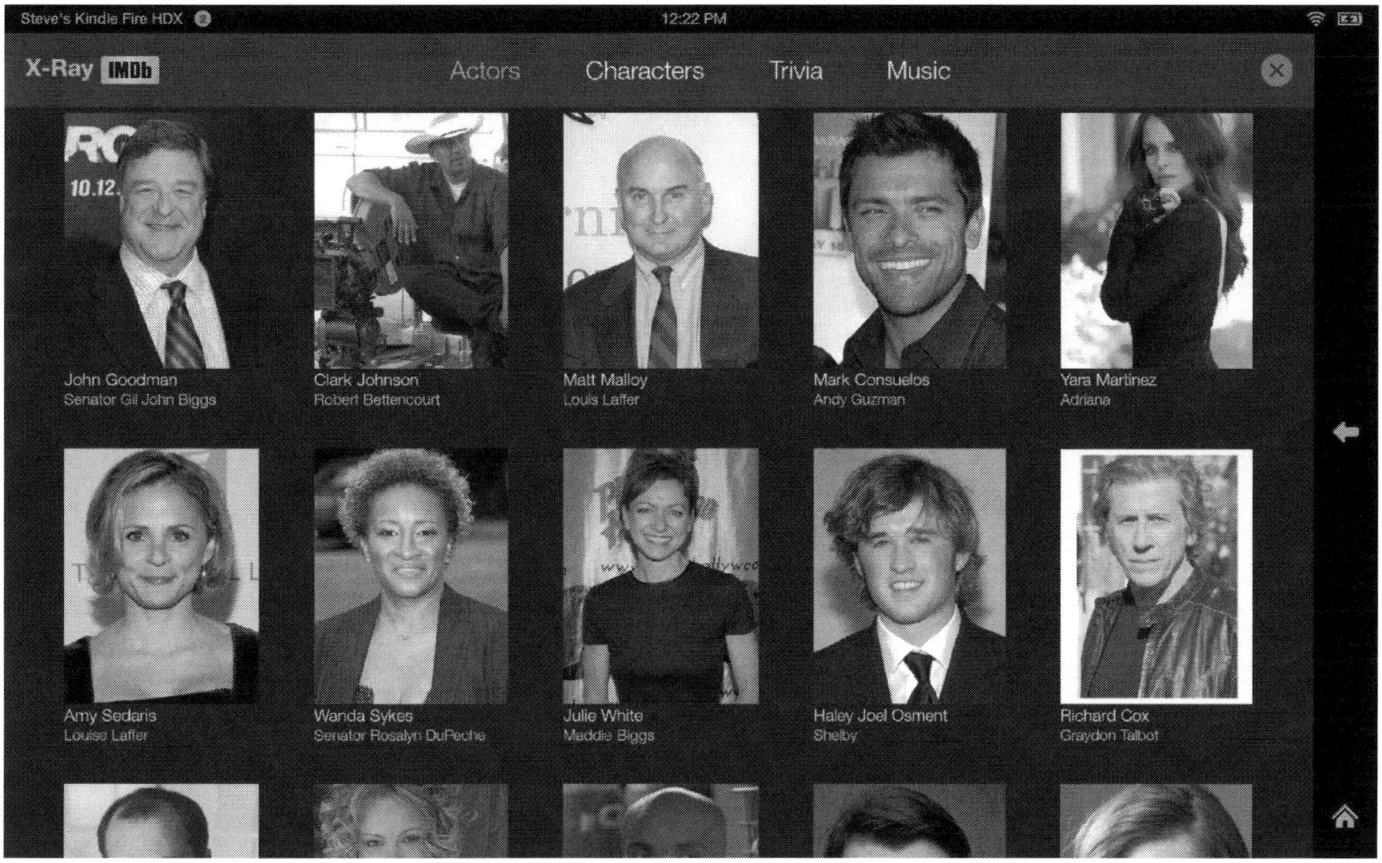

Access to Prime video is included with annual Prime memberships, 30-day Prime trials, and paid Amazon Student memberships. Prime video isn't included for Student memberships in the six-month free trial period, Amazon Mom memberships after the 30-day free Instant Video trial, or for guests of Prime members.

Using X-Ray for Movies and TV shows

While watching a compatible video title on your Kindle Fire HDX or Wii U, you can view extra information about the video using the X-Ray feature—including actor biographies, trivia about the title, and more. Using a Kindle Fire, tap anywhere on the screen during playback to access X-Ray. To hide X-Ray, tap a part of the screen outside the window. Using a Wii U, select the "Cast" menu on your TV display.

In addition to Prime video, you can also rent or buy video from Amazon's store. Non-prime movies cost about $3 to $8 for a 48-hour rental.

Setting parental controls

You can set parental controls on Amazon's Instant Video settings page on Amazon's website, amazon.com/video/settings . In addition to the webpage, you can access parental controls directly on Kindle Fire, Fire TV, and Xbox consoles.

Also, you can require a PIN for access to videos when using Amazon's website, PlayStation, Wii, and some TVs.

For more information about Fire TV parental controls, visit bit.ly/ParentSetup .

To set Instant Video parental controls using Amazon's website:

1. Visit the Instant Video Settings webpage, https://www.amazon.com/video/settings .
2. In the **Parental Controls** section, enter a five-digit PIN.
3. Under **Viewing Restrictions**, you can elect to restrict video playback depending on the ratings category. You can also choose which devices you want to restrict viewing on.
4. Under **Purchase Restrictions**, you can choose to govern purchases on all your devices (except the website, Kindle Fire, and Fire TV, which have purchase restriction settings specific to that device).
5. Click **Save**. Now your PIN will be required for video purchases.

Video ratings categories

Amazon uses the ratings classification system from the Motion Picture Association of America and the TV Guidelines Organization guidelines.

Downloading Prime videos

You can download some Amazon video titles, which enables you to view the video later without using a wireless connection.

1. Connect your Kindle Fire to Wi-Fi.
2. Browse or search for a video title and open its description page. A **Download** button appears with eligible titles.
3. For movies, tap **Download**. For TV shows, tap the down arrow next to the episode you want to download.
4. When the download is complete, access the video by opening the video library on your Kindle Fire. Tap **Video**, then tap **On Device** to find and play the video. In most cases, you have 15 to 30 days to begin watching the downloaded video. Once you begin playback, you have 48 hours to finish viewing.

3 ► USE THE KINDLE OWNERS' LENDING LIBRARY

Amazon Prime members can borrow one book per month from the Kindle Owner's Lending Library with no due dates. Not all books are eligible for borrowing, and you must use a Kindle device for borrowing (not a Kindle app on your smartphone, for example).

Here's how to borrow from the lending library using a **Kindle Fire**:

1. From the Home screen, tap **Books**.
2. Swipe from the left side of the screen, then tap **Kindle Lending Library**. You'll see a display of eligible titles.
3. Make your selection, then tap Borrow for Free.

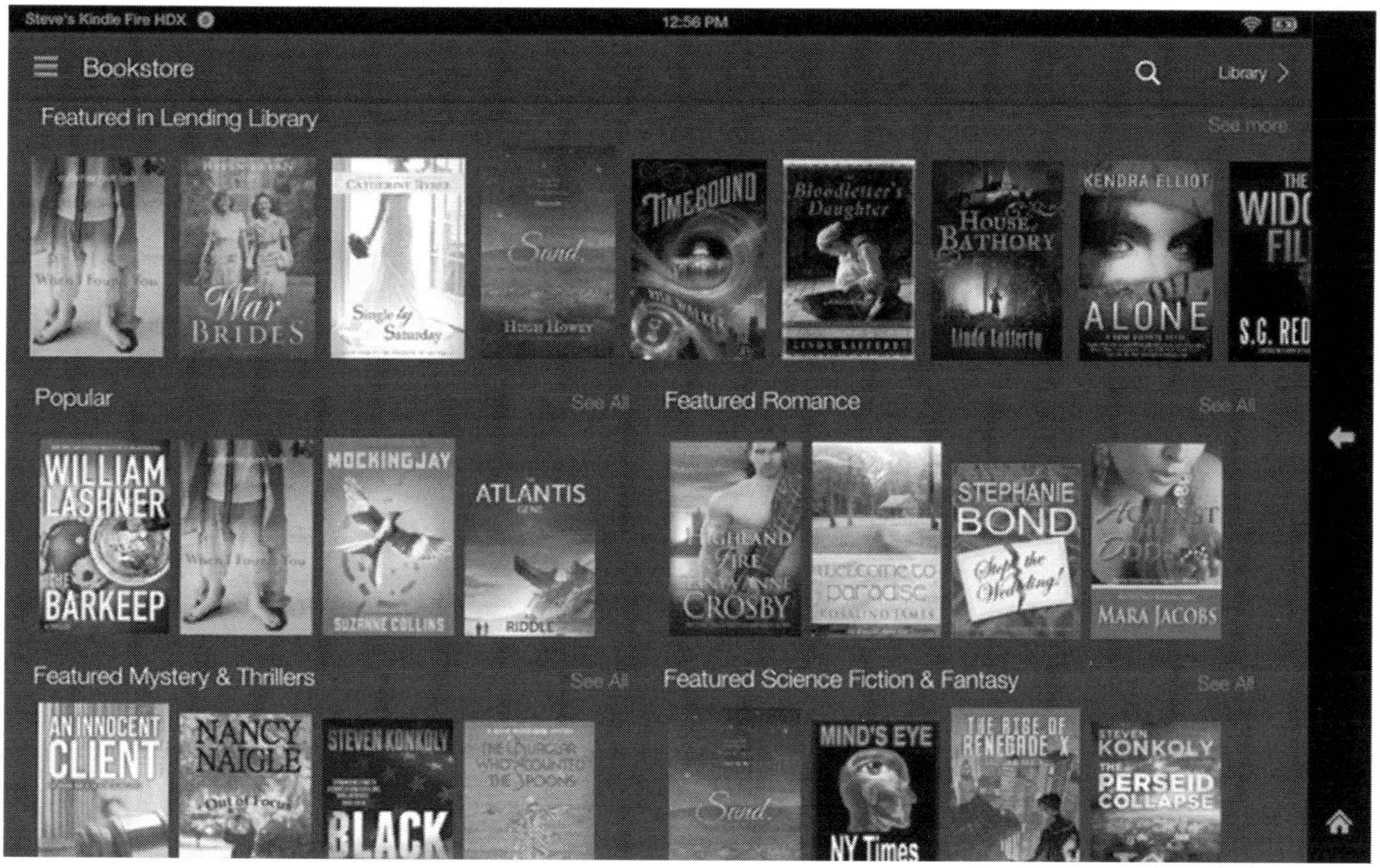

Here's how to borrow from the lending library using an **E-Ink** or **Paperwhite** Kindle:

1. On the home screen, click on the shopping cart to visit the Kindle Store.

2. On the top navigation bar, click the menu button on the right edge.
3. From the pop-up menu, click **Kindle Owners' Lending Library**.
4. Browse the books eligible for borrowing.
5. Select a book to reveals its description page. Click **Borrow for Free**.

How many books may I borrow and for how long?

You may borrow one book at a time, with no due dates. You can borrow a new book as frequently as once a month, and you'll be prompted to return the book you're already borrowing.

If I finished a book before the month is over, can I borrow another book?

If you've already borrowed a book in the current calendar month, you must wait until the next calendar month to borrow another book. Unused borrowing eligibility doesn't roll over into subsequent months.

Borrow Books From a Public Library

You can borrow Kindle books from the websites of local libraries and have them sent to your Kindle or reading app. Although a Prime membership isn't required, this method of borrowing books deserves a mention here. About 11,000 U.S. libraries offer Kindle books. Just like regular library books, Kindle books may be loaned for a specific period of time. Since only one copy of a Kindle book may be loaned at one time, there might be a waiting period before you can borrow a popular title.

1. Confirm whether your library branch carries Kindle books. Visit your library's website or visit Overdrive, the company that handles library Kindle lending at www.search.overdrive.com
2. Obtain a library card and PIN from your local library.
3. Search for Kindle books at your library's website.
4. At checkout, sign into your Amazon account, and select your Kindle device.
5. Your Kindle should receive the book automatically. If not, sync your device manually.

Sharing Kindle books among family members

The "easy" way to share Kindle books with other family members is to register multiple Kindle devices with the same Amazon email address. For example, in my household, each Kindle device—mine, my wife's, our young daughter's—is registered to my Amazon email address. My account is used for all Kindle purchases, so each book we buy is automatically shared among all the Kindles in our household. It's convenient, but the adults in the household must take care not to purchase content that is inappropriate for youngsters.

Another way to share Kindle books is to use the **Family Library** function. Family Library adds more control—books may still be shared, but certain content may remain private. For example, you can link two accounts to a single device, which can enable a spouse and partner to share books. Meanwhile, those two folks can jointly supervise and control the accounts of as many as four children.

The only slight drawback with Family Library is that it takes some time to set up. For more details, visit bit.ly/FamilyLibrary .

4 ▶ LISTEN TO PRIME MUSIC

Just as Amazon is shaking up the online TV and movie world with its Prime Video, it's making a splash in the music world with Prime Music. If you've ever used a streaming music service like Pandora, Spotify, or Rhapsody, you'll be glad to know that Prime Music is included in your Prime subscription and provides more than a million songs , along with hundreds of playlists (A playlist is a list of songs that can be played in sequential or random order.) You can enjoy the service free without commercial interruptions.

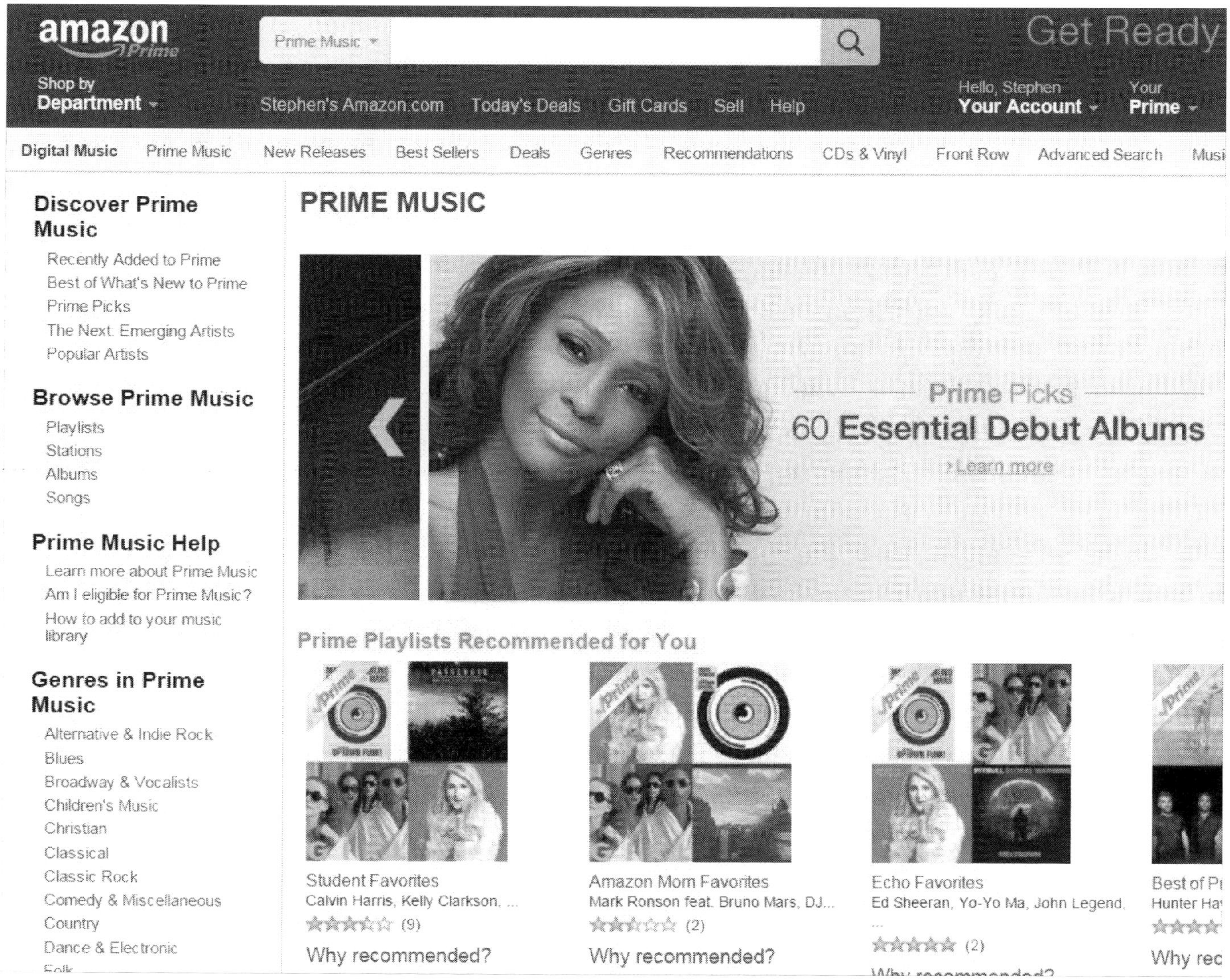

Above: The home page for Prime Music, http://www.amazon.com/PrimeMusic .

Prime Music is like a personalized radio station—the more you use it, the better it gets because it learns your musical preferences. You can easily rate songs with a thumbs-up (if you like it) or thumbs-down (if you hate it), and this fine-tunes the musical you'll hear later.

You can listen to Prime Music on Kindle Fire tablets, Apple and Android tablets and smartphones, PC and Mac computers, and using Amazon's Prime Music Library on the Web player, located at bit.ly/MusicCloudPlayer .

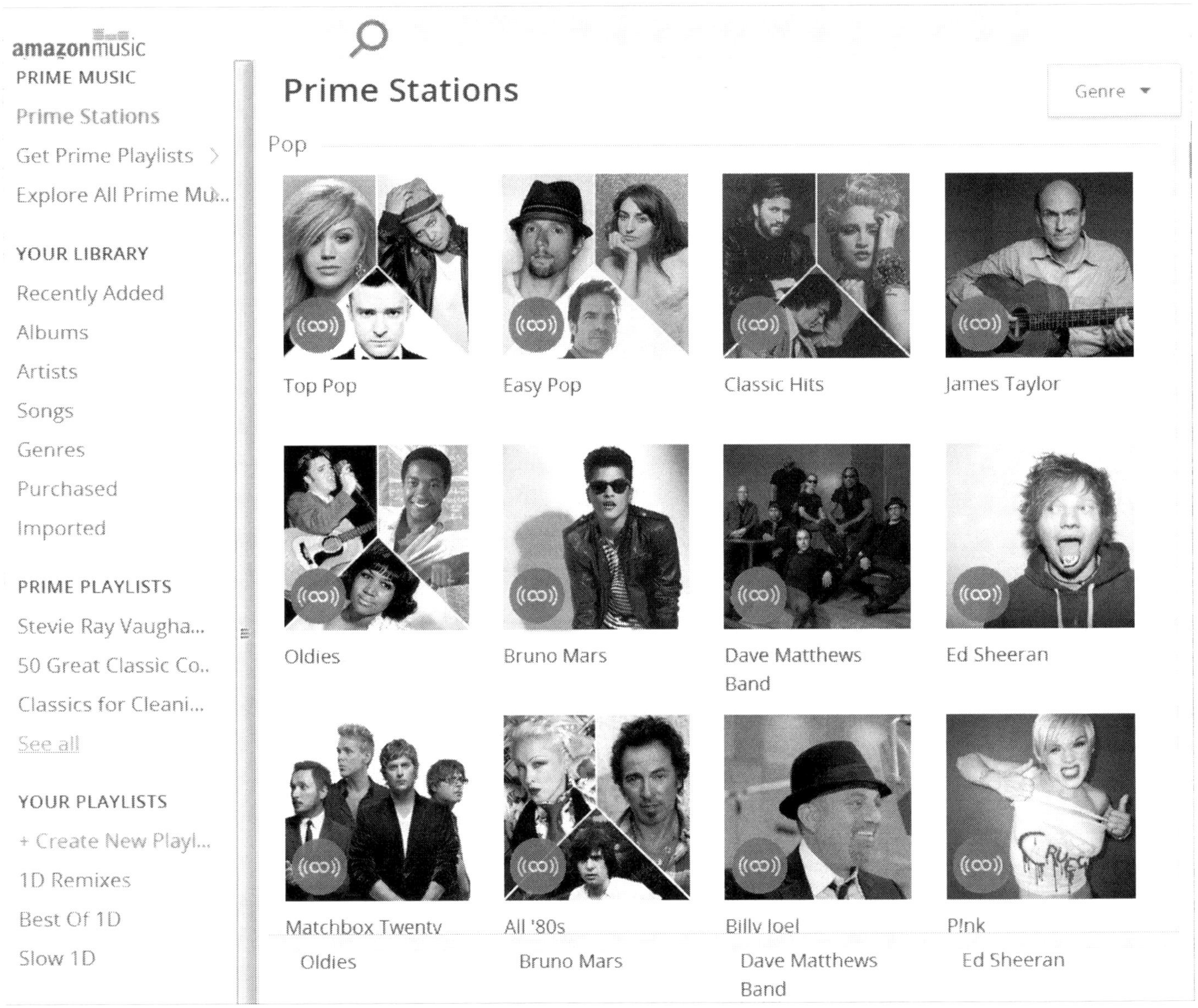

Above: A view of Prime Music Library on the Web player, https://www.amazon.com/gp/dmusic/cloudplayer/web

Another big plus with Prime Music is your unlimited ability to skip past songs you don't want to hear—some competing services only allow you to skip over a few unwanted songs per hour.

Getting started

Visit Amazon's Digital Music Store, amazon.com/mp3 to browse or search for songs, playlists and albums. A "Prime" logo will appear with eligible titles. You can also filter search results to show only Prime-eligible music. To add a song, album or playlist to your library, select +**Add**, +**Add album to library**, or +**Add playlist to library**.

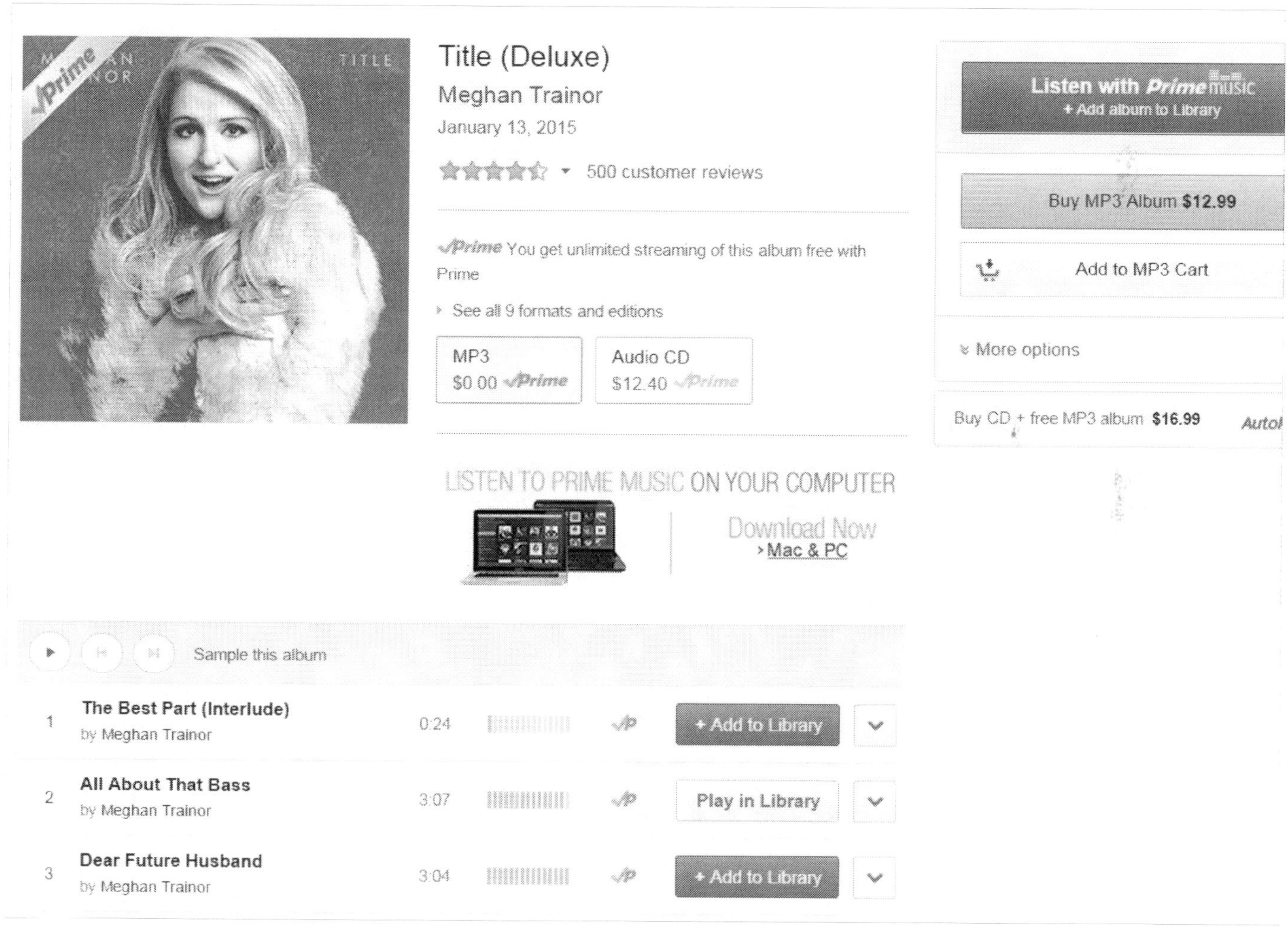

Above: After selecting a Prime-eligible music album, buttons appear to enable you to add the album or individual songs to your library.

After you add Prime music to your library, it shows up under several different headings of your library—artists, song, genres, albums—alongside any other digital music you may have purchased from Amazon. You can also filter your music library using the criteria **Recently Added**.

Using the Amazon Music app

If you use a mobile device to listen to music, you'll be interested in the Amazon Music application available in the Amazon Appstore or Google Play. Search the appstore for "Amazon Music" then follow the instructions on your screen to install the app and sign in with your Amazon account.

After you've installed the music app, swipe from the left edge of your screen or tap the **Menu** button to access your library.

You can also install a widget for the Amazon Music app on your device's home screen (a widget is an icon that serves as a shortcut to an app). Using the widget, you can play music from your home screen or play songs in random order. To install the widget, press and hold an empty part of your screen, tap **Widgets**, then drag the widget to the desired location.

For more information about the Amazon music app and links to the versions for different types of devices, visit the page bit.ly/AmazonMusicApps .

Downloading music for offline playback

Using the Amazon Music app, you can download Prime music to your mobile device, enabling you to play music without an Internet connection.

To download music:

1. Search or browse your library for the Prime song, playlist or album you want to download.
    - Kindle Fire tablets: For songs and albums, tap the overflow menu (three vertical dots) next to the desired title, then tap **Download** from the menu. For playlists, tap the desired playlist, then tap the **Download** icon.
    - Apple devices: For albums and playlists, tap the desired title, then tap the **Download** icon. For songs, tap the three vertical dots beside the song, or on the Now Playing screen, then tap **Download**.
2. You can access your downloaded Prime music by switching from **Cloud** to **Device**. (On Android and Apple devices, the location is called **Cloud Library** to **Offline Library**).

Your **Offline Library** shows any iTunes music or playlists you've already stored on your device, in addition to music you've downloaded to your device from your Cloud library. To view your library, tap the **Menu** button and select **Your Library**.

Using Prime music stations

Prime stations provide streaming music that becomes personalized as you use them. You can "like" and "dislike" songs and skip past unwanted songs as often as you wish.

From Amazon's website, click on the **Prime Music** tab and select **Prime Stations**. Pick a genre, such as Pop, Classic Rock or Country, and select a station to begin listening. If you like the song currently playing, tap the **Thumbs Up** icon, and you'll hear similar songs in the future. Tapping the **Thumbs Down** icon will skip the song being played and remove it from your station.

You can also tap the +Add button during playback to add the current song to your music library.

Creating a playlist in your music library

To create a playlist in your music library:

1. Visit the Playlists section and tap **+Create New Playlist**. (On Kindle Fire tablet, it's simply a + icon.
2. Enter a name for your playlist and tap **Save**.
3. Select the songs you want added to your playlist.
    - On the Web, click **Add to playlist**, then select playlist name from the drop-down menu.
    - Using the Amazon Music App: Select **Done**.

Viewing song lyrics

You can view lyrics for many Prime songs while listening to music on your Kindle Fire tablet or Amazon Music app for Android or Apple. Eligible songs have a **Lyrics** label next to the title, and an **X-Ray** or **Lyrics** panel on the Now Playing screen.

Lyrics display line-by-line, synchronized with the playback. You can tap or drag the lyrics panel to expand or hide the lyrics.

To view lyrics on Amazon Music for PC or Mac, click the album icon or the lyrics badge next to the playback controls.

Importing your own music

If you already have a personal collection of music, you can use the **Amazon Music Importer** to add that music to your library, so you can play it from all your connected Amazon Music devices.

To import:

Visit your music library, https://www.amazon.com/musiclibrary using your computer.

On the left menu, click **Upload your Music**. If you're prompted to install the Importer, follow the instructions on your computer screen.

After you've opened or installed Amazon Music Importer, click **Start Scan** to search your iTunes and Windows Media Player libraries for songs available for importing. To search elsewhere on your computer, click **Browse manually**, which can take quite a while.

After the Importer has located your music, click **Import all** to add all the files to your library. Or click **Select Music** to identify which songs you want to add.

Amazon allows you to import up to 250 songs at no cost. With an Amazon Music subscription costing $24.99 annually, you can import as many as 250,000 songs. For more information, visit Amazon's Manage Your Cloud Subscription page, https://www.amazon.com/clouddrive/manage

Keeping access to your music library

There are a few scenarios in which you won't have access to your Prime music. First, the selection of available Prime music changes continuously—new titles are constantly added, while some are dropped. Discontinued titles will remain listed in your library, but are greyed out and can't be played. To regain access to those titles, you'd need to purchase them from Amazon.

Secondly, if your Amazon Prime membership expires, you will no longer have access to the Prime music you've added to your library.

Thirdly, music you've downloaded to your mobile device through the Amazon Music app won't be immediately available if you haven't used the app while connected to the Internet for the past 30 days. In that case it may take about 10 minutes for you to regain access to the downloaded music after you reconnect with the app.

And finally, Prime music you've downloaded for playback offline is deleted from your device if you sign out of the Amazon music app.

Sometimes, if you can't find the music you're looking for, you merely need to refresh your library. Open the app menu (swipe from the left edge of the screen or tap the **Menu** button), select **Settings**, then select **Refresh** at the top of the screen.

Deleting music from your library

You can delete music files from your library using a Web browser on your computer.

Visit your music library, https://www.amazon.com/musiclibrary .

Check the boxes next to each file you want to delete.

Select multiple songs by checking the box next to the first song to be deleted, press and sold the **Shift** key on your keyboard, then check the box beside the last song to be deleted. This highlights all songs between the top and bottom song selected.

Free and Discount Kindle books, all you can eat!

Kindle Buffet is a daily website that features a hand-picked list of great Kindle books being offered free that day. Includes mysteries, romance, science-fiction, horror, non-fiction and more. Today's bestsellers and yesterday's classics. You may never need to pay for a book again! See for yourself by visiting www.KindleBuffet.com

kindle buffet

Free and bargain books, all you can eat!

Page 1 | Page 2 | Page 3 | About / Privacy | Past Issues | My Books

Free Kindle books & bargains for Friday, May 22, 2015

3 Sleuths, 2 Dogs, 1 Murder (The Sleuth Sisters)

Contemporary Fiction
Author: Maggie Pill
FREE

When Retta's "gentleman friend" is accused of murder, the Sleuth Sisters take on the case. Winston Darrow is a charmer, but his secrets create trouble that spills onto Retta, Barb, Faye, and even police chief Rory Neuencamp. Someone is out to get Win, someone he claims is the real killer. While Retta admits Win is less trustworthy than her daffy Newfoundland dog, she insists he's not a murderer.

Dogs become an issue when Faye rescues a mutt she finds hurt on the road. Though Barb isn't a fan, she can't refuse Faye's request to keep the homely, ill-tempered Buddy. Retta, though doubtful about adopting strays, is determined that Faye's dog and her Styx will be

Small Space Organizing: A Room by Room Guide to Maximizing Your Space

Crafts, Hobbies & Home > Home Improvement & Design
Author: Kathryn Bechen
Regularly $12.99, Today $0.99

While we may admire the spacious rooms in large homes we see in magazines or on TV, let's face it: most of us don't live in rambling estates. Instead, we live in homes, apartments, or condos with small rooms and even smaller closets. But you can enjoy an organized, beauty-filled life no matter what the size of your space. In this practical book, you'll learn how to

perform a room-by-room audit of your space to see if it's functioning at its best make

Made in the USA
Coppell, TX
04 November 2026

11287988R00020